Tongues of Men and Angels

Tongues of Men and Angels

Poems by

Joy Roulier Sawycr

Kelsay Books

The author gratefully acknowledges Southern Methodist University Press for permission to reprint four lines from Vassar Miller's 22-sonnet cycle, "Love's Bitten Tongue," from *If I Had Wheels or Love: Collected Poems of Vassar Miller* (Southern Methodist University Press, 1991).

Cover photograph by Karen Davies (Tintern Abbey, Wales)

ISBN 13:978-0692661284

Kelsay Books
White Violet Press
www.kelsaybooks.com

Acknowledgments

My sincere thanks to Andrea Dupree and Michael Henry for long ago creating the vibrant community that is Lighthouse Writers Workshop in Denver, and for the many good writer and poet friends I've been honored to meet there.

Special thanks in particular to Lighthouse poets who read and commented on these poems in workshops, either individually or collectively, especially David J. Rothman, Jody Sorenson, Roger Wehling, Anna Napp, Chris Ransick, Malinda Miller, June Inuzuka, Marie Ostarello.

Thanks, too, to Renee Ruderman, Catherine Wiley, and Alice Dugan for their very helpful comments on drafts of "Following the Piper."

I'm so grateful for my poetry teachers, both past and present: Ray Gonzalez, Galway Kinnell, William Packard, Lorie Hartmann, Sonia Sanchez, Michael J. Henry, Kathryn T.S. Bass, Chris Ransick, David J. Rothman, John Brehm, Lynn Wagner, Jake Adam York, J Diego Frey.

I'm privileged, too, to have learned so much from a fine assortment of visiting Lighthouse poets who offered poetry talks or workshops: Mark Irwin, Pattiann Rogers, Mark Strand, Thomas Lux, Mark Doty, Kim Addonizio, Major Jackson.

My deepest gratitude to Chris Ransick for nourishment and friendship, as well as for his generous and insightful help with this collection.

And most of all to Scotty, who is a beacon of brilliance, kindness, good humor, humility—also traits of the very best kind of writing—thank you. You are indeed chief of men sidled up to *The Tender Bar*. I am so blessed to share this life with you.

Of course, grateful acknowledgment is also made to the following publications where these poems or earlier versions first appeared:

Denver Poetry Map: "Plain Speech at the Tattered Cover Bookstore" www. denverpoetrymap.net

St. Petersburg Review: "Following the Piper: An American Elegy *I-VIII*"

The Bacon Review: "Italian Exile" and "German Chocolate Tetrameter Taste Test"

Torrid Literature Journal: "The Poem is Sold Out by the Horatian Heroes of the Eternal Boardroom," "The Poem Sends a Surprise Birthday Card to the Last Man Standing at the Bar," and "The Poem is Read on the Pont des Arts Bridge, Paris"

The Volta: Evening Will Come (A Tribute to Jake Adam York): "Death's Columbo"

Eight interpretative small box-pieces by abstract artist Margaret Withers of "Following the Piper: An American Elegy *1-VIII*" were featured at the NEXT Gallery, Denver, Colorado.

"Following the Piper: An American Elegy, poems *I-IV*" was staged as a performance piece at the Space Gallery, Denver, Colorado, as part of the Rocky Mountain Women's Institute Associateship showcase. Featuring actress and playwright Coleen Hubbard ("Cape Cod"); Denver Poet Laureate Chris Ransick ("Kansas"); performance poet Joy Roulier Sawyer ("Dallas"); performance poet and National Poetry Slam Champion coach Ted Vaca ("Chicago"). Video collage produced by LIDA Project artistic director Brian Freeland.

"Following the Piper: An American Elegy *I-VIII*" was selected as runner-up in the annual *St. Petersburg Review* contest.

This one's for
the good men in my life

Contents

No hand plucks them and no fingers can gather

These snowflakes melting so swiftly they dress

The air this moment their wannesss has stung

You, my God, lonesome man, Love's bitten tongue.

—Vassar Miller

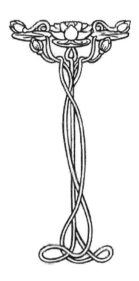

Italian Exile

The friend who fled for Tuscany one spring
arrived to find fine fields ablaze in bright
Barbera grapes, a succulent free-swing
of tangled vines and ripened fruit, a sight
so sweet my friend could scarcely bear to sing
his song of deep delight in prose. He'd write,
then throw away. Begin again. Erase.
But then the postcard came: *I tasted grace.*

The Poem Ponders the Ethics
of the Humble Armchair Psychologists

Do No Harm
hangs high upon our muted beige walls,
a tranquil manifesto of benevolence, and peace.

Welcome to our world of balance.

Of course, in times of destructive chaos
one must shun kinky hair, freaky locusts,
beating one's breasts in unrelenting anguish,

fits of uncontrollable poetic hyperbole
over beers at the White Horse Tavern.

Instead, we must work together quietly
and without fanfare, in dutiful service
to each soothing, helpful, spiritual word:

Do
investigate those who are fervent
as they may veil an agenda to evangelize

No
odd or dangerous stories, please,
as they disturb our denuded zen

Harm
only those who quarrel and question
our standardized quest for diversity

Sameness will ensure we are all on the same page.

We sincerely wish it wasn't necessary
to choose propaganda over poetry, to use
distortion to warn of difference's danger.

Yes, we address you, gentle reader,
and regret to inform you of a most
statistically-skewed observation of
the mean:

apparently, one must break the law again and again and again

for the sake of perfect order.

Plain Speech at the Tattered Cover Bookstore

There's a new title
on the old Lowenstein Theater,
deserted on Colfax at least twenty years.

The bookstore tip-toed from Cherry Creek,
where I once spotted skeletal women
toodling, tottering on Jimmy Choo's.

So how does this urban store read,
where East High skateboarders
sip Chai and flash dragon tattoos?

Inside, I wander down a narrow ramp
to an old orchestra pit,
theater posters pasted on walls.

"Death of a Salesman" played in the sixties,
Willy Loman lamenting in Denver
while Jerry Rubin burned flags back east.

Would I have chosen Willy or Jerry?
Probably Jerry. I would've fried flags,
certain protest beats plain words on paper.

Today, I slump into velvet matinee seats,
surrounded by hardbacks on stage,
ponder the plight of dear Happy and Biff.

Eye the jackets. Scan the spines.
Wonder what attention must be paid to
art.

The Poem Blanks Her Verses to the Good Ladies of the Underground Railroad

There is a cost we scarcely dare to say.
There is a price we pay for what is true.
We hold the keys of life and death with hope;
we teach the tongue to tell the toughest truth.

And what of men who cannot see the dark?
And what of those who will not hear our plea?
We leave the hearth of all we hold so dear,
and sit at meals with those who learn our hearts.

We share our bread with friends who risk their lives;
we risk our wine for those who find our friends.
We quilt a living sacrifice of love:
Our calico is all we bring of us.

And if we see that we are bound to die,
we'll save the few that we were meant to save.
We'll find a way to bleed such words of life
that all who read our faces will revive.

German Chocolate Tetrameter Taste Test

Ze world is full of *sturm und drang:*

bad writing with no lemon-tang.

So satire seems the sweetest trick

when feelings start to taste too thick.

Some bite, some wit, some saccharine break

should scotch emotions on the take.

Because the truest fact we feel

is when the gush of goo ain't real.

The Poem is Sold Out by the Horatian Heroes
of the Eternal Boardroom

Scorned and left roiling, ransomed, wretched lovers—
faithful to faith and fighting fear, but reeling;
burned by your branding, blistered raw and wringing
blood from my poem.

Sold out for power, priceless sacrifice of
pride, by those climbing greed's eternal ladders,
pulpits of prose, of deadness, death embroiled in
bored rooms of bizness.

Love is not angled, plotted, coiffed and cloying,
strategized simply, opiates of order,
powerpoint presentations, smoke machines of
heat with no heartbeat.

Blessed are the Germinating Meek

'Tis the season of winter as frost fills our pane,
of the sleek silver sliver of ice down our drain;
of the crisp powdered snow and whisp-fog of hot breath,
of the shiver and quiver of conjugal death;
of the sweet knotted buds of bright fruit underground,
of the birth of deep dreams of pure poppies unfound.
Oh, the wonder of weather is willfully wild—
for the colder the climate, the more we grow mild.

The Poem Sends a Surprise Birthday Card
to the Last Man Standing at the Bar

Can you be a woman writer

and wriggle static-free
from frayed designer labels
of "charming" or "brilliant" or "brave"—

you know, spy a *real* novelist
in the literary buffet line
who reads you up and down and sideways and finally sighs:

Damn, girl. You sure do make me wanna show-not-tell.

Can you be a woman writer
and shrug off the predictable frump and grump
and finger-wag of strident sisters—

you know, kick off sturdy lace-up shoes
of poop-brown protest, slide those
poems into sassy red sling-backs and sing:

Damn, girls. Come on, now. Even these couplets got legs.

Can you be a woman writer and disregard
archaic rules all square and angled,
all boxy and stingy and snarly—

you know, all "parceling out the joy"
in teeny eentsy-weeny
munchkin-sized portions?

Hey, boy. Wanna clue?

Say you left my house after *coq au vin,*
whistling, half a French silk pie
tucked snugly underneath your arm,
when suddenly you realized:

Well, now. There's more where that *came from.*

It's like that.

The Morning of the End of my Enlightenment

—a line borrowed from Jack Kerouac

The morning of the end of my enlightenment,
I will greet my husband like Carmen Miranda—
forget oil prices. I'll squeeze grapes to pay the rent.

The morning of the end of my enlightenment,
I will guzzle mint juleps on an Atlanta veranda—
dinner is served, dear time. Wonder where you went?

The morning of the end of my enlightenment,
I will croon Nat King Cole to a Chinese panda—
the upright uptight need their bamboo bent.

The morning of the end of my enlightenment,
I will pilfer all the library books on Alexandria—
plaster pages full of poems to Babylon I've sent.

Yes, on the morning of the end of my enlightenment,
 I'll phone Walmart to snag my pal, Amanda—
say, "Hey, is your birthday gift card spent?"
Note to self: give up enlightenment for Lent.

The Poem Eludes Writer's Block
by Teasing Her Favorite Allusions

So much unhinged
through rose-colored glasses
oblivious to thunder
beside the burning bush.

That freaking conehead
wedged his spoon
into my Ben & Jerry's
and would not care!

This Nabisco sampler of cookies
in my spam filter:
delusional red poppies
in a hot lime peyote field.

Shall I measure out my life in wine glasses?
Shuck my trousers, sport a bikini on your beach?
I'm telling you, pals, I can hear the Whiffenpoofs
singing within reach.

So here's a fat, wet kiss over your shining grave.
Everyone liked you. But no Brut for a non-brute gnu
like you. Muse, muse, my beloved—it was you.

Following the Piper: An American Elegy
November 25, 1960-July 16, 1999

I. Cape Cod

Ashes adrift at sea, we undulate free and brave

against the pull of midnight's tide. Are we lost?

Found out? Not here, not *now*. Pipers play on the graves

of scattered shells, fragments of the cost

of childhood's peace. Still, our white clapboard house

on the blued cliff promises home—and so much more.

In late spring, we sail on iced waters, douse

bonfires with red buckets rimmed with shore,

hold rumblings at bay. We lick fingers at pig roasts, barbecues,

sponsor sock hops on glassy gym floors of crinoline loves.

When seasons change so rhythmically, how can we possibly lose?

Daddy's desk is for crawling under, a castle for kids and doves.

   This is our only glimpse that fall before sight.

   This is all we know, or should: clean, unsifted daylight.

II. Kansas

This is all we know or should—clean unsifted daylight

streaming through cracked barn windows like milo haze.

One Friday before fall, I catch sight

of saluting combines, crisp wheat whisks razed

to the downy cradle of ground. It is a measured march

of harvesters, swish, swish, staccato beat

against the coronet sun. Silver rain pellets parched

ground, lightning drums copper fields. Farmers eat

fried chicken, mashed potatoes, chocolate cream pie,

sneak naps in humid hammocks hanging still.

After, poker games—but no ace cashes in. Lies

soak the air like lazy gin; wrinkled bills

      slide across wooden tables; Cuban cigar incense.

      Gray pigeons rest along our splintered fence.

III. Dallas

Gray pigeons scatter wildly from a splintered fence,

yellow roses twist around rusted nails, splattered paint,

a daisy droops in the fading sun. Knuckles tense,

relax. Tense again. Crackling TV men are patron saints,

black-and-white statues rolling marble tears, our static hope

for miracles, or love. When we bought the convertible ride,

we believed our scrapbooks could cope

with speed, or sound, or both. We never dreamed we'd hide,

slide down the slick back seat, clutch our heads,

murmur the wordless *no.* Too late to switch cars,

forget November, pretend we're brave. Now, the bed

never sleeps, the legend doesn't die, we parry with swords

      bearing no peace. Backward boots on a bone-bare pyre.

      The smoke of this flame twists higher and higher.

IV. Chicago

Smoke and flame twist higher and higher, thin flags

of ribboned sky, a chant gaining speed, and sound.

Napalm nights burn through summer days. We drag

bodies across lawns, broken fingers clutched around

guitars with crocheted straps. Hell, no, we still go, songs climb

this ladder down. Seven, four—matchstick numbers mark

our slow descent. Somehow, we mime

this war. Fingers erupt electric rage: the stark

difference between them, and us. Us. Never again like this,

never again the loud lullaby that soothes and berates.

The city's shoulders stoop, shattered by the kiss

of law and skull. Hard to breathe. Wait.

     Wait like the urgent shove of a miscarried child.

     Like a widow wailing at her lover's grave defiled.

V. Washington

Wait like a veiled widow. Wail for love's grave defiled

by a cheap gun served on a silver dish. Salute the train

slowly death-rattling by. Remember Memphis, musky and mild,

cloudburst of snipers, another hotel? Is it *done?* Now, feign

content. Even our silences are taped. So maybe

erase the sarcasm, ferret out the Jews. What's the point?

Ever jeered a jester for trying too hard? We

grow weary, paint freedoms that won't disappoint

the patrons. Stick to the cardboard, the flashlight,

the black gloves and upraised fist. Read *Newsweek, The Times.*

Marry in Greece. Hoard gas. Pick a fight

with Billie Jean King, your wilted wife. Don't rhyme

      poetry, above all. Paste ideas random and pale.

      Forget words. Don't even try if you think you'll fail.

VI. Hollywood

Forget poetry, ok? Just a random idea. You won't fail

to find fulfillment here—we'd *love* to be your fan.

Or, are you tired of the image? Try economics or law, sail

sleek yachts, throw pink Frisbees, walk the dog, tan

your backside at the beach. Or listen to hip hop,

taking acting lessons, watch *Cheers.* Understand?

Reality check: So you didn't graduate at the top

of your law class. Maybe the Image is land-

locked in our souls, like a checkered Big Boy.

Feel free to deflate. Sip a foamy beer at the bar,

critique the Lakers, pore over Polaroids of *moi.*

Ride breezy bikes, ditch confining cars.

No more blood, impassioned speeches.

No one can live the love the Image teaches.

VII. New York

Why can't we just love the image and all she teaches, redress

her in red satin and white pearls, head straight

down that sleek catwalk and admit we won't confess

our crooked flesh, impatience at our kingdom's wait?

Believe me: We'll soon drink tea on your heirloom tray.

There is talk of fluffing pillows on our queen beds.

Even if we miss the stifling C-train, there is a way

home. Believe me. No matter what the cynics said,

immortality will drape her arms around us. Top hats

tip in Harlem, Park Slope, on Riverside Drive. Invisible

phonographs play under park benches where we once sat.

True love will kiss our hand with joy. It is livable.

      Engraved on the browning bark of green elm trees:

      Your East Village is drenched in lilacs. Believe me.

VIII. Martha's Vineyard

The east village drowned in lilacs, believe me,

when our ivory tower slid into the sea. Down, down it flew—

past the sock hop, the bitter bay, inflated images we still see:

wilted yellow roses, a pink suit, tiny pea coats in blue.

Falling like Icarus, a melting scrapbook, trailing beer,

barbecues, Cuban cigars, Polaroids and NYU law;

a dog named Friday, Wyclef Jean, a role in King Lear.

Caroline's love rolling through tobacco fields is what I saw.

This spiral a crackling reminder in static spin:

heaven scattered in seconds, a generation of gray

again midnight blue. Miscarried hope in

Harlem's womb, mockingbird's loud lullaby displayed.

    We followed our Piper Saratoga, its black convertible cost.

    Ashes, adrift at sea, undulate free. At last. And who is lost?

July 16, 2009

The Well-Storied Poem Deconstructs Betrayal

You superstitionistas keep your thirty pieces of certainty.

I turned my face away long ago, a poor pilgrim, a stranger
in desperate search of his ancient danger, remembering
how he felt that brutal bruise of a kiss again as he died.

How many Thursdays the dutiful peck on the check,
evening stung raw by betrayal, heart handled by harsh
hands heavy with the silver greed of the need to be right?

But unlike his Friday, never far from Sunday's surprise
splashing through shadows, cracking simmering silences
wide open with its sweet, hilarious, guileless laughter.

Stories are bought back, brought back, undone, retold—
pure kisses from a faithful friend, love's gambled gold
unsold, heaven's taste trembling on honeyed tongues.

The Poem Undergoes an Unwanted Explication

When the scientist lifts his cool trained eye
from the microscope, he says, "I'm sorry.
They are indeed spreading, and strange."

Funny. When I study my white cells
under the horn-rimmed lens of heart
smoldering speck into blaze

I see

gray fleck of #2 pencil lead
crinkled under rice-paper joint
third grade scrawled into left thumb

thin stream of Kansas sprinkler
peeling mud-speckle from elbows
freckled child pretending black

pearl-tipped straight pin
jimmying the lock
of a creamy gardenia corsage

one steady sperm
swimming upstream
nailing a neglected egg

how my mouth desperately misses yours
through sterile steel bars of facts
concrete 4 x 4 of *now*

how
white cells morph and morph
and multiply, billows of marshmallow

fluff, smothering pillows that swallow,
swallow hard—

renegade gag of mutants
who subdue, strangle, seek

to lay me down to sleep.

Forgive Me, Poetry

For it was the Eve of St. Agnes
since I last confessed my trembling.
One musky twilight, surrounded by

lush *shushhh* of sprinklers at dusk,
I knelt down in a deserted garden,
beads of lilacs pressed between palms.

I asked forgiveness, again and again,
for the tale of destruction my tongue
was surely shaped to tell—

ashen fallout flaking fertile fields,
radioactive incense roiling
through fevered, smothered dreams;

brutal concrete plagues, word-famines,
years when no hot sap streamed through
thick thighs of sycamore and elm.

Forgive me, poetry, forgive me
for I knew not what I did to you

I then sang praise for seed-words of life,
breathed gratitude for gardens grown wild —
for goodness gifted me a new tongue.

Over and over, until my mouth
formed faint syllables, fashioned voice,
whispered true in a thousand listening ears:

Forgive me, poetry, and thank you—
please show me who harmed us
please show me how I harmed you

for your kindness leads to the healing path

Year after year, as the harsh hail hit
the delicate petunias, hurling them
drunken and reeling across clay pots,

I'd press my face against blurred glass,
rocking, mourning, keening like wind,
violent tears washing the floorboards.

I refuse to even speak your name.
So you're absent? Abstaining? Allow
lovers to be battered and barren?

for your long silences are deafening

Only in hope's embrace did poetry hush, hold,
hide me safe in brooding shadow. *Poetry, ardent*
angel wrestling through darkness until dawn.

Poetry, laming and claiming, naming his own.

Forgive me, poetry, and thank you—
in presence, in absence, in anger and delight,
in faithfulness and my need for forgiveness

you are the only one I've ever loved

So find me, lose me, faithful friend, furious enemy,
desperate lover. Find me in blinding sunlight, boiling
thunder, beneath snowfall's sheer sheet of frozen grass.

Find and lose and find me until I am found.

For in sorrow's slumber I dreamed I awoke,
then spoke—mouth gloriously alive, tribe
joyful, fed fresh fruit from the healing tree.

Morning glories, entwined, beckoned—
bright faces of shining bliss. Budbursts
of blackberries astonished sweetened tongues.

So please forgive me,
my lovely love, my untamed language,
my fierce and wild and unrelenting heart.

Forgive me again and again, as I forgive you—

for I am nothing if I cannot kiss
what surely seeds and fruits forever,
and never fails.

For they shall beat their swords into ploughshares

Death's Columbo

When we dare draw hope's last refrain of breath,
and breathless from love's past, we glimpse our best
bright longings now laid bare; and when thin death,
his face dissolved, grows pale when paired with rest
from sheer albino fear; when our grave's guest,
arrested for grand theft, his shortened stay
payday—the way death's sting discerns our test
of life, and will not underlord our day:
We'll call it a night's work. But until then, we play.

The Poem is Read
on the Pont des Arts Bridge, Paris

The spirit of the lover is not the bitter wind but a breath,
lips pressed on trembling lips, murmuring *live oh live oh live.*

The spirit of the lover is not the brash microphone but an ear,
your ear touching my ear touching ear touching. Touching.

The spirit of the lover is not the harsh accuser but a question:
Why do you flee such fierce longing, all the day long?

The spirit of the lover is not the cruel whip but a caress,
your face the treasured map, many years in the tracing.

The spirit of the lover is not the dull strategy but a poem:
these fresh, fragrant peonies/blooming sensual delight.

The spirit of the lover is not the caustic cynic but a comforter,
wrapping you with downy wings, warm and gracious arms.

The spirit of the lover is not the feeding frenzy but a taste:
For lo our unforgiving winter is over. O taste and see.

The spirit of the lover is not the brassy lock but a key,
freeing you to flee, forget—or open love wide.

45

About the Author

Joy Roulier Sawyer is the former poetry editor and contributing editor for the *Mars Hill Review,* a national journal of arts and culture. She has published poetry in diverse publications such as *Books & Culture, Christianity & Literature, LIGHT Quarterly, Lilliput Review, New York Quarterly, Ruminate, St. Petersburg Review, The Bacon Review, The Other Journal, The Volta, Torrid Literature Journal,* and others. She was a recent runner-up in the annual *St. Petersburg Review* contest, as well as awarded a Rocky Mountain Women's Institute associateship for her performance poetry. Joy received her MA from New York University, where she won the Herbert Rubin Award for Outstanding Creative Writing. She has taught at the University of Denver and Lighthouse Writers Workshop.